Speaking Their Language

Or
Evangelism Without The Jargon

Heather Sutherland

DEDICATION

This book is dedicated to Iain who has always believed in and supported me.

Also to Grace and John who wanted to see their names in print – I love you both!

Contents

Foreword:

"I believe that one of the biggest challenges facing the church in Scotland today is the ability to learn how to be missionaries in our own culture.

Missionaries need to learn the language of the people we are going to. In our setting this means we need to learn how to stop speaking 'church' and start speaking 'spiritual seeker'.

This is exactly what this little book is all about"

Alan McWilliam

(Minister at Whiteinch Church of Scotland and Chairman of CLAN Gathering)

Introduction

It was my Dad's birthday and because this was his 70th, the family presented him with a laptop. 'Welcome to the 21st century'! What happened next was the grandchildren were telling him that he needed to: "boot it up", "sign on", "double click", "copy & paste", " move the mouse", "tweet", "FB" them etc. etc. etc.

For most of us, this sounds funny, because we know what these terms mean. However, can you remember a time when words like 'download', 'website', or even 'email' were not part of your vocabulary? How did you feel when people around you were talking about these 'things' that you knew nothing about? Or what about 'going forward', and 'blue-sky thinking'? These are phrases from management speak that are filtering into every-day use, but can you explain them?

In churches we also have our own language. We on the 'inside' know what we're talking about, but people who are not 'one of us' yet have no idea what we're on about! This book is to help us Christians unlearn the jargon we've picked up on our spiritual journey.

The example we have for *not* using 'religious' language in our spiritual conversations with people is Jesus. If you look at the parables in the gospels, you'll find Jesus telling stories to people using words and images from their everyday life. So he used language that would be easily understood by the people that he was trying to communicate with. Now, admittedly, not everyone understood what he was saying (but that's why we've got the explanations that he gave to the disciples). However, this should encourage us because there will be people who just 'don't get' what we're saying.

So how do we put this into practice in real life?

On my first adventure of doing outreach at a university students' union, a young guy came to our team with a dream. The interpretation of the dream basically was that God was calling him to be an evangelist. The team's dilemma wasn't working out what the dream meant, but what we said to the dreamer. After a few minutes we told him that "... something was going to make a big impact in his life and that he would find himself telling other people about it." The guy left and the team left a little bit deflated as though we hadn't done a good job. This feeling was exaggerated shortly afterwards when the same guy came back into the room and joined the line for another team: we genuinely thought he wanted a second opinion.

A few minutes later he came over to our team and said: "I hope you don't mind, but you were so good, I've brought some of my friends in to have their dreams interpreted too!"

What an encouragement for us!

On the other hand though, God is very good at introducing Himself to people! At a large New Age Fair one young woman wanted us to tell her who the man was in her dream that she was to marry. Instinctively, the team knew it was Jesus, but it didn't feel right for us to tell her that. Instead she was told to close her eyes and ask the Creator who this man was. After a short while she opened her eyes and told the team about this Prince with 'magical powers' who told her that he'd created the whole universe and loved her very much. So we chatted about this Prince who came to earth two thousand years ago who died and rose again because he loved her. Then the young woman said, "It was strange, when my eyes were closed I kept hearing the name 'Jesus', but I didn't want it to be Jesus!" Her upbringing as a Catholic meant that she had a preconceived idea about who Jesus is, but the way He introduced Himself to her blew these preconceptions away and we were able to talk to her about this 'real' Jesus.

During evangelistic conversations, you need to be very aware that you are part of a *trialogue*, not just a dialogue! What do I mean by this? Well, it put it simply, it means that as well as engaging in conversation with the person who is in front of you, you also need to be listening to God and asking His guidance on which words/phrases would be most useful to use in this particular conversation. To begin with talking to people in this way, using the words God prompts us to use, may seem clumsy and un-natural but can I encourage you to stick with it? You will eventually find that the results are worth it as you engage people in conversation that go to deeper levels than you were previously able to do.

Missionaries to our own Community

As Alan McWilliam mentioned in the foreword, it may be helpful for us all to think of ourselves as missionaries. If God sent us to a foreign country where they speak a language that is different from our native tongue, one of the first things we would need to do would be to learn the language of the people that we were going to in order to communicate with them. Why do we do things differently on our own doorstep?

We are surrounded by people who have very little or no knowledge of what being a Christian is about and how it is relevant to them, but many times we insist in trying to communicate with them in a language that they do not understand. Yes, on the surface we may still be speaking English (or whatever your native language is) but we are using a technical, church version of the language that they do not understand.

Over the years, I have attended many training sessions for various evangelistic events and quite often the training involves quoting passages of the Bible to explain to the person why becoming a Christian is a good move for them to make. However, let's go back to the example of Jesus. When did he quote scripture at people?

A close look at the gospels show us that he did this when he was confronted by Satan in the desert during his forty days in the wilderness, when he was dealing with the religious leaders of the day and also on occasions with his close disciples.

Quite often we will try to show people who are not yet Christians that they need to be born again. Yes, this is biblical, but look at the context of the conversation Jesus uses this phrase. He is talking with Nicodemus, an important religious leader of the time. Being born again was a theological concept that Nicodemus would have been familiar with because the idea was found in the Talmud. For Jews in the first century AD, life here on earth was viewed as a gestation period, like being in the womb. True life does not begin for them until they are 'born' into heaven. So when Jesus said this to Nicodemus, he was using a metaphor that Nicodemus would immediately understand.[1]

---

[1] If you wish to follow up this point then I recommend this link as a good place to start **www.hadavar.org/drupal/content/you-must-be-born-again**

However, in 21st century western cultures the term 'born again' is most commonly used in connection with Evangelical Christians (as in "born-again Christians") If we start to talk to someone with no church background about being born again, the image that is brought to their mind is something which is very different from what we are trying to talk to them about.

Jesus only mentions our need to be born again once, but this is the most common passage used in evangelism!

Please note: I am not saying that we don't need to be born again – we do! What I am saying is that we need to learn to express this concept in a way that our friends, family, neighbours, work colleagues etc. understand and can relate to.

We need to learn to speak the language of today. The majority of people we interact with on a daily basis, or when we do specific evangelistic events, do not understand parables of sheep or fig trees so we need to find new ways of communicating God's truth to them. We do not want to change the message of Jesus to suit the people we are talking to, that could lead us into heresy or false teaching. We can though, change the approach we use to communicate with them.

If you study the way that Jesus encountered people you will find that he was kind, loving and demonstrated God's power to those who were not believers. He did not use the popular verses from the Bible that we use in evangelism today. This is something that will need to be gone into more fully elsewhere and is not the topic for this little book, but I am hoping that it will get you thinking and searching the gospels for yourself to find out more about Jesus' style of evangelism.

Word List

Ok, so this is probably the section that you bought this book for! It's in alphabetical order so it should be fairly straightforward to use.

Here are a couple of disclaimers though:

1) This list is not meant to be exhaustive. I have taken phrases from a variety of denominations so as you go through the list you may find some phrases that are new to you. You might also find that there is a phrase you use around church regularly that is not included in this list – my challenge to you here is to come up with a way you would explain the phrase to someone outwith the church.

2) Neither is the list meant to be the only way you can use non-religious language suggested for each 'religious' word or phrase. If you can think of a way to say it differently/better/more natural for you then be my guest!

3) Language is changing rapidly so the suggestions I have made here may seem dated in a few years from now – so why not update them yourself?

These suggestions are just to get you thinking...

How to use the list:

It might be right for you to simply read through the list and memorise some of the definitions I've offered.

However, you could also use it as a team building exercise for your group before you go out on outreach together.

One suggestion would be to give a team member a religious word and then get them to say what the word means in non-religious terms!

Alternatively you could just talk to each other, but have some kind of forfeit for anyone who uses 'religious' terms.

The possibilities are endless!

A

A thief in the night: coming at an unexpected time or way

Abide: to remain—don't change what you're doing—stay close to God

Above reproach: honest; trustworthy

Adoration: deeply expressed sincere love; devotion

Amen: That's right! I totally agree

Angel: spiritual being

Anointing: You have special characteristics. People seem to be drawn to you. You are uniquely gifted.

Apostle: spiritual man with great authority and leadership; a spiritual father who sacrifices much for those he leads and loves

Apostolic: something or someone with the traits of an apostle

Armour bearer: a person who helps and supports a leader, they can be trusted

Assignment: there is an evil plan against you

Atonement: Jesus took responsibility for our mistakes so that we can get to know God better without those things standing in the way

Authority: You are a very take charge kind of person. You have clout. You are able to influence others. You are about to gain greater control of some situations in your life.

B

Baptism of the Holy Spirit: new power from God; Let the Spirit fill you with God's new light and love.

Baptism with water: a picture to remind us that we leave some old habits behind when we start to follow Jesus

Be fed by the word: we receive spiritual insight from reading the bible

"Believing for" (something—a promise): waiting with expectation for God to do something specific

Bible: God's words, ancient holy writing

Birthing: God has given you a gift or new idea and you are going through a process to bring it to life

Bitter root: deep-seated negative issue or attitude that keeps you from growing spiritually, often related to unforgiveness

Blasphemy: showing extreme disrespect about God and spiritual things; cursing God

Bless you: all the best to you; good thoughts for you; best thoughts of love and God's goodness toward you; you are in my thoughts and prayers;

Blessed assurance: having a relationship with God that brings great confidence

Blessing: good things; something good is coming your way benefits; advantages

Blood of Jesus/ blood of the lamb: depending on context, refers to Jesus' death or what He accomplished by dying on the cross

Body of Christ: Christians, churches; all Christians; Christians in general; people who consider Jesus their leader or authority

Bondage: being trapped or restrained, dealing with a situation in your life where you feel like you have lost the power to choose

Book of Life: (as in "is your name written in the book of life?") – the place where God has recorded the names of his children; those who will go to heaven

Born again: to have a spiritual awakening or spiritual experience; turn the control of your life over to Jesus

Bounty: abundance, goodness

Break bread: eat together

Breakthrough: you are about to get past something that has been holding you back or limiting you

Brethren: like-minded people; other Christians

Bring forth: to produce or create something

Brother/sister: a fellow believer in Jesus

Building relationship: getting closer to people, making friends

Burden: Concern for; solicitous of; care for; being praying for

Burdened for someone/something: a spiritual or emotional weight that a person experiences on behalf of others; is often relieved by praying for the situation; see also **prayer burden**

Burden bearer: someone who by their nature is often sensitive to what other people are going through and tends to pray for them; someone who prays a lot

Burning desire: wanting something in a way that gets you really excited.

C

Call of God: destined to do something; something you have been chosen to do

Call on your life/call of God: you have an appointment with destiny; you have a greater purpose in life

Call things that are not as though they are: talk about the things you sense or imagine as though you can see them actually happening and it will help them come to be

Calling: what you were created to do; something you are uniquely gifted to do

Calling down fire: when Christians think God is mad at what they are mad at; wanting God to punish, when he probably doesn't agree; compare to **righteous anger**

Carnal mind or thinking: a point of view, or a way of thinking, that excludes spirituality; it is also thinking that tends to focus on one's self

Carry your cross: do what it takes to stay in the process of becoming all you were created to be; don't stop because it got difficult

Chastise: to correct or reprimand; tell someone off

Check in your spirit: when something does not seem right, it isn't something you know by what you think or what you can see – it is the feeling you get inside that something isn't right

Christian walk: spiritual journey

Church: spiritual community

Cleansed whiter than snow: we can get the chance to start clean slate with God

Cleansing refining, healing; some things need to be changed; give up some old habits

(to) **Come forth/coming forth**: something is happening right now, perhaps something new and long awaited

Come into agreement: when two people have the same view about something to be done – Jesus used it to say that we can get more accomplished together than we can alone

Coming against (a spirit or a person): taking a side against darkness, or darkness working through someone

(being in) **Communion (with God)** God wants to be closer to you; see also **intimacy**

Contemplative prayer: a spiritual practice of being quiet and focusing on God

Conversion: complete spiritual overhaul; when someone decides to follow Jesus

Convicted, conviction: becoming aware of things in your life that need to be changed

Corporate worship: expressing honour to God (often with singing) in a group setting

Covenant (entering into): made between two people or between God and a person; it is a promise or a commitment to act in definite ways

Covered with the blood/washed in the blood: what you have done wrong has been forgiven because of Jesus' dying on the cross

Covering: protection, security,

D

Daily bread: spiritual food; also anything we could possibly need that God provides for us

Dark night of the soul: a time you may go through in your spiritual journey, it can feel disorienting or lonely, it is a time where you are relying less on other things and coming to rely more on God

Deceived: condition in which a person cannot distinguish (spiritual) light from darkness, you've been lied to, either by a person or spiritual being (see **demons**)

Declaration (declarative prayer, "declare a thing"): a statement that is positive and strong and usually indicates you have cut off other options

Deliverance: removing any obstacles that are keeping you coming into your full destiny in God

Demons: negative forces; something negatively influencing your life

Desert places: a time in your life that feels dry or lonely

Die to yourself: refusing to feed selfish whims and desires, can include doing what you know is right rather than what you might want to do

Discernment: the ability to distinguish good from evil; able to see beneath the surface to the root of an issue;

Disciple: a student

(To) **disciple:** to mentor or teach someone, usually referring to the teachings of Jesus

Divine appointment: a meeting or relationship that God made happen

Do not trust in yourself: learn to trust God more than your own feelings

Downcast: depressed; bummed; down and out

Download: helpful insight that God suddenly brings into your mind; v. the process through which God gives insight, borrowed from computer terminology, not a bible term

Drunk or filled with Holy Spirit: overwhelmed or filled with God's spirit/presence

Dry bones: something that is lifeless

E

Edify: to encourage, build up, support or strengthen

Edification: learning new things; encouragement

Elder: someone with spiritual maturity who has a leadership role in their church, they help with many of the practical aspects of taking care of people

Election: the mysterious way God chooses those who choose him

Elements (as in elements of communion): the bread and wine (or juice) that represents Jesus' body and blood; used during a church service, eaten when people who follow Jesus take time to remember his last meal before dying on the cross; see also **eucharist**

Encounter: experience where God reveals something about himself to you, sometimes in dramatic ways see also **power encounter**

Enemy: dark or negative forces; Satan

Equipped: prepared, trained, ready

Eternal: continuing forever

Eternal life: live forever

Eucharist: the bread and wine (or juice) that represents Jesus' body and blood; used during a church service, eaten when people who follow Jesus take time to remember his last meal before dying on the cross; see also **elements**

Evangelical: refers to followers of Jesus who believe that the bible is inspired by God and that Jesus' teaching about life and death are true

Evangelism: influencing others for the Creator, telling others about what it is like to follow God and encouraging them to get to know him better

Evangelist: someone who influences others for God, can mean someone who does it on a regular basis or has special gifting from God in this area

Evil: negative forces; spiritual forces that are determined to bring about your downfall.

F

Faith: trusting in what you can't see yet; just believe; have faith—believe that things will work out; don't give up; you feel like there is more to life

Fall of man : a time near the beginning when the first people God created chose to disobey; the first time a man did anything wrong – it represents how we all can tend to want to do our own selfish things

Fall on the rock: choose to cooperate with the process of growing to spiritual maturity – even when it seems hard – because it is easier than resisting God

Father God: Creator, God. (Note: the word 'father' can be difficult for some people, especially if their experiences of father or father-figures have not been good, so tread carefully with this one initially. See also the Names of God section of this book)

Favour: good things are coming your way; God is smiling on you

Fear and trembling: something you are apprehensive about doing

Fellowship: friendship

Filled with the Spirit: feeling up to date with God, as open as you can be, knowing him as well as you can, able to hear him and only able to do his stuff with his help

First fruits: when you give to God don't give the leftovers, give your best and show that you honour him

Fivefold ministry: God knew it was a big job to help all the people who follow him grow up and work together so he created five special kind of leadership roles to help with that (see: "apostle", "prophet", "evangelist", "pastor", "teacher")

Flesh: your own desires as opposed to what God wants for you

Forerunner: A person who is one of the first to know, tell or do something, thereby making it easier for others to do the same e.g. a spiritual pioneer

Free will: God gives you the right to choose if you believe in him or not

Free gift of God: God doesn't expect you to earn this, he wants to give it to you because he loves you

Fruit: character changes; evidence of change in your life from God

Fruit of the spirit: good characteristics in your life from having a relationship with Jesus through the Holy Spirit

G

Generational ties or sin: a negative connection through your ancestors that is blocking good things coming to you; negative things in your family, dad or mom, grandparents, etc. that are affecting your destiny

Gifts or giftings: You have special ability. Something you are naturally good at, a God-given ability. You have special ability to _____. There's something special in your personality.

Glorification: making Jesus famous, acknowledging his worth

Glorious: beautiful, wonderful,

Glory! Awesome!, cool!, way to go God!

Go to the nations/call to the nations: see missions

God: Creator, Spirit of Light & Truth (see Names of God section of this book)

God's Heart: understanding the way God feels about something

Going to the next level: making a significant positive change in spiritual maturity, God can trust you more and give you more responsibility

Good report: happy result, often after prayer for a difficult situation

Gospel: message of Jesus. Good news that can help you.

Grace: Things are going to be easier. Someone is going to cut you some slack.

Grave clothes: baggage from the past that can stand in the way of living a new life

(The) **Great Commission:** An imperative that Jesus gave his followers to teach everyone everywhere what he taught them, convincing them of his great love

Grieved: deeply saddened or disappointed

H

Hallelujah: wonderful! great! awesome!

Hard ground: Things have been difficult for you. You have been through a lot.

Harvesting: bringing in the proof, reaping what you sow, seeing the end results

(Jesus is the) **head of the body:** refers to Jesus being the brains and ultimate leader of all his followers everywhere

Healing: Things are going to change for the better. You are recovering from something. You are recovering from _____.

Heart: As in *I have a heart for you or getting God's heart:* I really care about you. To love someone, or something, like God does.

Heart like David: You are like David of the Bible. He was small but tough and he loved God.

Hell: a place of great suffering and pain

Holiness: do things right; get it together with your spiritual life; staying pure

Holy: pure

Holy Ghost/Spirit: Creator, God's spirit, his essence;

Hope deferred: waiting so long for something you have wanted that you start to feel discouraged

House of God: church building

Humanistic: self-reliant, excluding the possibility of spiritual answers

I

"I don't get a witness about…" – just say you don't know!

"I'll pray about it": I will talk to God about this

"I'm just blessed to be doing this!": another way of saying, "I like to help," or "I'm happy to be here."

Idol(s): any person, activity, or thing that people seek out for security and comfort that isn't God!

Impartation: to freely give to someone a good spiritual gift that God that God has given to you

In Jesus name: because of the authority that Jesus has; doing something as Jesus would

In the flesh: a generally negative phrase referring to behaviour that isn't inspired by God, but comes from a person's own ideas and desires, and often fails to accomplish anything spiritually positive or lasting

In the world but not of it: loving people without being influenced by what they do that is harmful to themselves and others

Intercede: pray

Intercede/intercession: It's more than just a quick prayer but to keep asking God to answer a prayer for someone or something.

Intimacy: personal relationship with God, deep understanding, very close

I've been released/I've not been released: either the person is free to do something or not, depending on what they believe God is permitting

J

Jezebel: refers to someone who is not a team player, who often tries to manipulate behind the scenes and control others

Jubilee: time of great freedom and happiness

Judas spirit: backstabber

Judgment: trouble

Judgment seat: a time in the future after your life is over where there is a review of your life and the choices you have made

Justification: changed life because of Jesus dying on the cross

K

Kill the old man: refusing to give in to old ways of doing things that don't acknowledge God's ways

King: God

King of Kings and Lord of Lords: God is the ultimate ruler, God has the ultimate authority, other people have authority of their own only because God allows it

King's kid: I know that God has everything in control and loves me so I don't worry because he will meet my needs

Kingdom of God: God's domain, everywhere God is in charge/control

L

Labour: work very hard, do your best

(The) **last days**: the time period between the last time Jesus walked the earth and next time he will. No one knows how many last days there are, though people try to guess.

Lay hold: to grasp or understand; also to fulfill a significant goal in one's life

Leading/felt led: Directed to do; prompted. "Felt like I should."

Lift up: pray for, talk to God about

Light of God: truth, also, all that God is—his greatness, goodness, rightness and love

Live by faith not by sight: seeing life the way God does

(The) **Lord's supper:** see **communion**

(The) **lost**: refers to people who are far from their spiritual home and God. (Note: People who don't know the love of Jesus do not like being called lost. It is better to say, "Those who are not Christians." or "People who don't personally know God's love.")

Lucid dreaming: being in a dream and being aware that you are dreaming, having an ability to influence or change the outcome of your dreams

M

Mandate: a purpose or goal that a person has

Manifest: someone or something's true nature is strongly made obvious; can be positive or negative

Mantle: something you have been created to do. You have a special purpose in life; a unique gifting; special ability from God; You are naturally gifted to _____. You may have always felt that there is more to your life_____.

Marketplace: places people work; business world

Milk v meat: easy to swallow or understand (milk) versus something more difficult to understand that requires more thought or time to chew on (meat)

Mercy: God's kindness and gentleness with us, comes often when we least deserve or expect it

Milk and honey (as in "land of milk and honey"): God wants to take you to a place where he can give you good things,

Ministry: something you have been chosen to do to help others; a destiny; an assignment from God

Missionary: lifestyle approach that people choose to help others get to know Jesus, even if it means moving to another country, and becoming immersed in a new culture

Mobilize: to get things moving in the right direction

N

Night season: When you sleep!

O

Office: relates to the special leadership roles as discussed in fivefold ministry – for a person to hold an office they would function consistently, have maturity and have great authority in that role – not many "hold an office"

(The) **old man**: our old way of living, self-centered, self-destructive, apart from God's love and help in our lives, unhealthy old habits or desires

On fire for God: excited about what God is doing

On my heart: I've been thinking about you. You have been in my thoughts.

Open doors: opportunities

Open heaven: Your mind is going to get much clearer. Answers are going to come to some questions that you have.

Overcomer: someone who has learned to depend on God's strength instead of their own

P

Pastor: someone who cares for people; leader of a church

Pearl of great price: the things of God have the greatest value, like the most expensive jewel

Pentecost: For followers of Jesus, the day that God's spirit was given to them to help them do all that Jesus asked them to do

Perseverance: stick with it even when things are hard

Pharisee: a person who talks spiritually, but behaves as though they haven't met God

Plank in eye: someone who can't think about things clearly because of their own issues

Portal: spiritual door or passageway

Possess a broken spirit or a contrite heart: be humble, open, and willing to learn

Possess the land: see **take the land**

Power encounter: experience where God reveals something about himself to you, sometimes in dramatic ways

Power of prayer: the amazing effects of talking to God about our pain and problems

Praise: be thankful or happy; appreciation; gratitude

Pray: talking and listening to the Creator; talking with God

Pray/prayer: meditate or meditation; reflect or reflection; communicate with God

Pray through: pray more than once about, until it seems like it's going to be OK

Pray to receive Jesus: ask Jesus to become like your best friend

Prayer burden: a problem that I'm concerned about and am talking to God about; also the feelings I have about the issue or person I'm praying for

Prayer closet: place where you talk to God regularly; not a literal closet, just a private place no one else knows about

Press in: be intentional, be focused on getting to know God

Principality: strong evil power, capable of influencing large territories and populations of people; also called **territorial spirit**

Proclaim: to say out loud, as opposed to inside your head

Promised land: term for anything wonderful that God has promised you; may require waiting and once received, more responsibility to maintain in your life

Promotion: being recognized for greater spiritual maturity

Prophetic act: a physical action that is like a picture of something you believe will happen

Prophecy: spiritual insight; deeper understanding; get a message or 'premonition' from God

Prophet: one who sees and understands spiritually, someone who does it on a regular basis or has special gifting from God in this area

Prophetic: see and understand spiritually; insightful, have a premonition from God; visionary

Prostrate/prostration: lying on the floor, stomach facing down, while expressing love for God

Protocol: A specific procedure, or order, in which things should be done.

Proverbs 31 woman: a capable and industrious woman

Pulpit: podium in a church; may also represent the speaker's responsibility to teach God's truth accurately and with integrity because of the influence he/she may have

Purity: doing what is right; staying away from things that may be bad for you

Pursue the Christian walk: become a Christian; find out more about the message of Jesus

Putting on the new man: living your life through God's power and spirit

Q

Quicken: I was reminded of— Just popped into my head; I remembered.

Quickening: to make alive, excite

R

Radical: enthusiastic, committed, resolved

Raise up: to promote someone, give more responsibility according to a person's spiritual abilities and maturity

Ram in the bush: unexpected provision or supply from God

Rapture: when Jesus returns and takes people to heaven

Reap what you have sown: some things you have done may come back on you; there is a price to pay; what goes around comes around

Rebuke: to correct someone

Redeem the time: make the most of your life and abilities; regain time you might feel you've wasted

Redemption: change for the good; salvage what has been lost

Refiner's fire: a time of spiritual cleansing, a difficult, but rewarding process to help you become more pure

Religious spirit : where someone may try to control your behaviour, typically specifying numerous do's and don'ts that are supposed to make you appear further along spiritually

Repent: ask God to forgive you and don't do it again

Repentant heart: to really be sorry and ready to ask God to forgive you; to come to a place where you are really sorry for things you have done wrong

Restoration: when God makes things new in your life, as though you had never lost or broken anything, especially your heart

Resurrect/resurrection: come back to life; big-time change; new life; metamorphosis; transformation

Retribution: revenge, getting even

Run the race: keep going, don't quit;

Revelation: new insight; get clarity on a situation; some questions will be answered for you; gut feeling(s)

Reverence: respect, honour, love

River of life: in the flow of things God is doing

righteous anger: being annoyed by the same things that anger God, such as injustice, hate, ignoring the poor, etc.

Righteousness: doing what is right

Road to righteousness: the spiritual journey to God

S

Sacrilegious: words or actions that intentionally show extreme disrespect for the things or practices of God

Saints: people who believe in and follow Jesus

Salvation: receiving forgiveness of your sins through Jesus dying on the cross; a spiritual awakening with God

Sanctification: grow spiritually; process of allowing God to change you

Sanctify your soul: you need to grow and mature spiritually; there is a higher justice; now is a time to look at, or deal with your issues

Sanctuary: safe spiritual place; building where Christians meet to express their love for God

Satan/demon(s): something negatively influencing your life; negative forces

Saved: spiritual; turned the control of your life over to Jesus; had a spiritual experience with God

Saved by grace: we get a new spiritual life that is not based on what we do—it's just because God loves us

Scripture: the bible

Sealed: your relationship with God was made secure

Season: period of time

Second heaven: the spiritual alleys where the dark spiritual agents hang out, a spiritual place surrounding earth where dark spiritual forces attempt to oppose the things of God

Secret place: a place you create in your life and in your heart where you can be very personal with God, a place where you and God can be real with each other

Secular: word used by some to describe things that are not sacred or spiritual; for some there is no difference

Seek fellowship with the Holy Spirit: allow the Holy Spirit to personally guide you; get a close relationship with God through God's Holy Spirit

Seek first the kingdom: make your priority the things of God; follow God first and other things will fall into place

Seeker-sensitive: refers to church services that are designed to make people who have never been to church feel comfortable

Seer: person who sees the spiritual realms, either in their spirits or with their own eyes.

Set captives free: a quote from Jesus; refers to something he promises to do for those who are stuck, discouraged, alone and without hope

Set free: peaceful state of being where the knowledge of God's personal love, affection, and protection is believed and enjoyed

Shekinah glory: an experience where God can be felt very present and very near, it fills your heart with wonder

Shepherd's heart: You are a leader. You are compassionate and concerned about others.

Signs and wonders: incredible acts that point to God

Sin: something that isn't right, an action that may have caused pain or a negative consequence; behaviour God doesn't like

Sinful nature: condition we are born with prior to having a spiritual awakening with God

Sister/brother: a fellow believer in Jesus

Speak in tongues: to talk in a spiritual language that God gives to you

Speak the truth in love: I need to be honest with you, but I don't want to hurt you.

Share: tell your story

Slain/slain in the Spirit: spiritual experience where a person is wiped out by the presence or activity of God; person may fall to the floor or lay on the floor

Soaking: positioning yourself physically, emotionally and spiritually in a quiet state in order to experience a deeper awareness of God

Sow into the kingdom: giving your time, energy, money, and abilities to what God is doing

Speak things that are not as though they are: seeing and saying things from God's perspective; i.e. where someone is going to be someday, not where they currently are; encouraging someone spiritually

Speak to your heart: communicate to your emotions and spirit more than to your mind

Speaking in tongues: speaking a Spirit-inspired language (or languages) that followers of Jesus may use when speaking to God

Spirit man: the innermost part of a person; our deep connection with God

Spirit of (   ): an overarching attitude that influences a person's behaviour; may be positive and influenced by the spirit of God, or negative needs example or something

Spiritual covering: a person or an organization that looks out for someone; will cover his or her back if necessary; when you are mentored by someone who can help guide you; getting in community; see also **covering**

Spiritual food: information that is going to be helpful in your spiritual journey

Spiritual gifts: special characteristics; uniqueness; you make a difference

Spiritual inheritance: all the good spiritual (and regular) things that God has determined to give you, can also refer to special abilities passed down through your family

Standing in the gap: talking to God on behalf of others I care for

Standing on the word: believing what the bible says is true; looking and waiting for God to demonstrate what he promises

Steadfast: stable or constant; consistency; stay on course; stick with it

Stronghold: something holding you back; obstacle; hindrance; in a rut; unseen obstacles that are holding you back from your destiny

Strongman: something opposing you or holding you back; spiritual resistance.

Stumbling block: obstacles to your spiritual growth

Submission: may be a heart attitude of love and obedience to God, or a team player approach to others who have responsibilities greater or lesser than yours

Surrender: ceasing to live life on one's own terms; giving up doing what doesn't work anyway

Sword of the Lord/Sword of the Spirit: a term for the bible; based on its ability to give insights to help you clearly separate right choices from wrong choices; Bible verses that help you grow spiritually

T

Take it to the altar: leave it with God, trust him with an issue's outcome

Take (or possess) the land: accepting something significant that God has promised you; this may involve greater commitment to maintain, or greater responsibilities in your life

Tarry: this is a place you should stick around for a while

Teacher: one who has a special ability to make difficult or mysterious things about God clear

Territorial spirit: strong evil power, capable of influencing large territories and/or groups of people; see **principality**

Testimony: the story about how God has impacted your life in some cool way

Testing: a difficult time that reveals our priorities and our heart attitude toward God and others; when times are tough and we have an opportunity to grow in character

Thanksgiving: happy or thankful

That which is hidden: something unknown; another way of saying, "I don't know."

Third heaven: heaven; place where God dwells on his throne

Tithe: a 10% portion, giving a part of your income to a ministry

Tongues: Spirit-inspired language (or languages) that followers of Jesus may use when speaking to God

Transformed: changed from the inside out

Transgression: wrong things that we have done

Transportation: unusual spiritual experience where a person may be physically moved from one location to another by God

Traveling mercies: having a good, safe trip

Trinity: refers to the mysterious three-part aspect of God's nature; he is Father, Jesus, Holy Spirit, yet he is one

U

Unction: compelled (by God)

Unequally yoked: when people have different views it is hard to work together

Under conviction: feeling the need to change something in your life. It may feel similar to guilt but it propels you to take positive action to change

V

Vex my spirit: become upset

Vision: (okay to use this word in some contexts); clarity; seeing things in a different light; getting some questions answered; getting perspective; change of perception; seeing a picture in your mind

Visitation: God comes close & spends time with you; can be dramatic & life-changing

W

Walk your talk: live according to your values; do the things you say

Warfare: when spiritual light and darkness clash

Watch and pray: be aware, know what you are up against, but talk to God about it and trust him

White-washed sepulchers: insult that Jesus used against his religious enemies. People who pretend to be something they are not.

Wilderness: a time when things are not very clear; difficult times; hard times; the pits

Wisdom: good advice; knowing the right thing to do; smart counsel

Witchcraft: spiritual forces that are not good for you

Witness: tell your story; talk about the difference God has made in your life

Word from God: spiritual insight; message from the spiritual realm;

Word of God: the bible

World/worldly: things that are not spiritual, thinking in terms of physical things that are seen as opposed to God's spiritual world

Worship: may refer to (1) a single church service, (2) only the music at the service, or (3) how a Christian gives their everyday life to God

XYZ

Yoke of bondage: a connection to something or someone that has become oppressive

Zeal: excited or enthusiastic; you seem to have a lot of drive

Names of God

As you step out and start doing evangelistic events, you will find that you come across some people who react very negatively to words we, in church, use to describe God. There could be a whole range of reasons for this, so it may be helpful for you to go out equipped with other names you could use instead of "Father God", "Jesus", "Saviour" and "Lord".

Please note: I am not advocating deception, but in the Bible God has given us hundreds of His Names and aspects of His character that we hardly ever use.

Have you ever considered that referring to Jesus as 'Good Teacher' may have a greater impact on the person you are talking to than using 'Lord'?

Another approach you might want to adopt is to use some of the Hebrew names for God. (This can work well if you are talking to people who could be classed as being interested in the 'New Age' as these names sound 'spiritual'). Adoni, El Shaddai, Jehovah Jirah, or Jehovah Rapha are just a few that you could use in this context.

This takes you back to the 'trialogue' I mentioned in the introduction of this book. When you're talking with a person you can be, at the same time, asking God which of His Names would make the most impact on this person.

In this section I have simply listed various Bible verses that refer to names or characteristics of God. Your job is to look them up, study them and then, when you are having a conversation with someone about God use one of these instead – easy! (It does not really matter which version of the Bible you use for this exercise as they will all give you different options to use. However, if you plan to use this in evangelistic enterprises you might find The Message or New Living Translation will give more 'user-friendly' options)

Here's an example for you:

John 8:12 – I am the Light of the World.

If you sense that the person you are talking to might have an issue with you mentioning the name Jesus, talk to them about how you connect with the 'Light of the World' and how this Light can dispel any darkness from areas in their life.

Some of them are obvious, others you may need to think about for a while. It really is that simple – but, to begin with, you might find it's not easy!

1. Genesis 21:33

2. Exodus 3:6

3. Exodus 3:14

4. Exodus 9:27

5. Proverbs 14:27

6. Psalm 23:1

7. Song of Songs 2:1

8. Isaiah 9:6 (hint there are 5 here)

9. Isaiah 11:2 (hint you can tease up to 7 out of this verse!)

10. Isaiah 43:15

11. Isaiah 44:6

12. Isaiah 44:8

13. Isaiah 45:12

14. Isaiah 51:12

15. Matthew 1:23

16. John 6:35

17. John 10:9

18. John 11:25

19. John 14:6

20. Acts 10:42

21. Hebrews 13:20

22. 1 John 4:8

23. James 1:17

24. Revelation 1:18

25. Revelation 19:11

26. Revelation 22:13

27. Revelation 22:16

These should be more than enough to get you started but please search the Bible for yourself.

Which of His names and/or attributes is God calling you to study, find out more about and use?

Resources

Websites

www.thedreamhouse.co

www.northatlanticdreams.net

www.streamsministries.com

www.lightlife.org.uk

www.lightproject.org.uk

Books

I Am Inheriting the Fullness of Gods Names
By John Paul Jackson

Prophecy, Dreams and Evangelism
By Doug Addison

Big Hearted
By Chris Duffett and Simon Goddard

Blogs

Whispers in the Night - Heather Sutherland

http://enupnion.wordpress.com

Be the Light - Chris Duffett

http://duffett.wordpress.com

About the author

Heather Sutherland is based in Dunfermline, Scotland.

She co-founded *The Dream House*, a ministry offering dream interpretation to anyone who searching for this service online. A growing part of this ministry is also to offer additional training in Dream Interpretation for anyone who has taken John Paul Jackson's courses in dream interpretation. She also teaches John Paul Jackson's courses via the *Streams* training centre based in Scotland, *North Atlantic Dreams*.

Heather is in some senses a reluctant evangelist, but she is passionate about connecting people, who have no interest in church, with Jesus. So as well as being the main trainer in Dream Interpretation for *Light and Life*, she part of the local leadership team for this them in Fife.

She is married to Iain and has two children, Grace and John.

17602405R00030

Made in the USA
Charleston, SC
19 February 2013